Contents

6   Hello!

8   Zöe's Monster Magic

12   Geth Gets Fired Up

16   On a Wing and a Prayer

20   The White Cliffs of Blue Peter

22   Brain of Blue Peter

24   Now You See It, Now You Don't

28   All About Andy

30   Bolivian Road Trip

36   Speed Demons

38   Flower Power

42   All About Zöe

44   Bahamian Bliss

48   Blast Off!

50   Geth's Best Beach Bag Ever

52   All About Gethin

54   Trek to the Top

60   Extreme Rugby

62   World Tour

63   Celeb Wordsearch

64   Behind the Scenes

66   The Story of Blue Peter

70   Their Last Adventure Together

74   Challenge Time

76   A-Z of Weird Animals

80   Half a Million Discs!

84   Me and My Costume Drama

86   Injury Time

88   Pumpkin Racing

90   Going Home

96   Geth Will Exterminate

100   Star Spangled Christmas Tree

102   Could it be You?

104   Meet Helen!

106   Meet Joel!

108   Pet Superstars

109   Credits and Answers

BBC Blue Peter

Annual 2009

Pedigree®

Published by Pedigree Books Limited, Beech Hill House, Walnut Gardens, Exeter, Devon, EX4 4DH.
Email: books @pedigreegroup.co.uk By arrangement with the BBC.

£7.99

HELLO!

Wow! It's been such an amazing year! We've climbed the tallest peaks in the UK, biked down the most dangerous road in the world and even fired a rocket on its way into space.

Not to mention the people we've hung out with: Richard Hammond, David Tennant, Same Difference, the Welsh rugby team (that was never you, was it, Gethin?!), Prince Charles, Kelly Holmes, the cast of High School Musical - even Miss Piggy and Basil Brush.

It's non-stop, it's sometimes exhausting, but life as a Blue Peter presenter never ceases to surprise. One minute you're converting a giant pumpkin into a boat, the next you're strapped to a plane about to go upside down for the first time. What we love most is discovering something new – and having fun together while we're doing it.

It also makes us really happy when we meet some of you, and see how you've been inspired by our adventures. To everyone who collected discs for our Disc Drive appeal: thank you. Please support our appeal this year if you can, which is all about getting meals on plates for children in the UK and around the world.

So it's been a great year – but also an emotional one. In January, we said goodbye to Konnie after over 10 years on the programme. And in June, both Gethin and Zöe bade farewell to what we feel is "the greatest job in the world".

Leaving is incredibly hard, but after so many awesome challenges, the time felt right.

The good news is that we have two new stars who've joined "the ship". You can find out a bit more about Helen and Joel at the very end of this book. In fact, it's great timing: Blue Peter is celebrating 50 years on air this year. We can't imagine a better moment for them to come aboard.

Enjoy the book – we hope you have as much fun reading about our adventures over the past year as we did having them!

PS Why not start with a quiz?
Have a guess what each of the pictures around this page refers to, and then go to the back of the book for the answers!

ZÖE'S MONSTER MAGIC

Yes, it really is me in that driving seat! This is the heart-stopping moment when I lifted a 5,000 kg monster truck several metres in the air to do a "sky wheelie" in front of thousands of spectators. But what happened next – and how did I get this far?

Turn the page to find out…

Name: **GRAVE DIGGER**

Cost: **£125,000**

Top speed: **100mph**

Jump distance: **30 metres**

Fuel: **Alcohol**

A few weeks earlier I had my first meeting with the Gravedigger, one of the most famous monster trucks in the world. I was expecting it to be big – but not this big. I'm 5' 7" tall, and, incredibly, its tyres were the same height as me.

The original Gravedigger was created back in 1981 in America, right at the start of the monster truck phenomenon. Since then, there have been nearly 20 different Gravediggers, each one bigger and better than the rest. Monster trucks, with super-strong suspension and extra-large tyres, were invented purely for the fun of seeing them crush ordinary cars and perform stomach-churning stunts. Tens of thousands of fans now attend "Monster Jam" events around the world – including the one in Cardiff at which I was to perform.

My team was driver Dan and his pit assistant Laurie. They taught me how to do a sky wheelie – that's when the truck lifts off the ground and flies through the air almost upright. But first, I had to learn how to drive the thing!

The main difference is that there's only one seat, and it's right in the middle. And you're surrounded by a metal roll cage to protect you at all times. What I really had to get used to, though, was how to manoeuvre it, and I had just two days to learn.

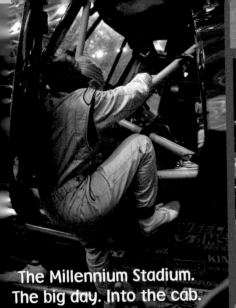

The Millennium Stadium. The big day. Into the cab.

Foot down – accelerate – on to the cars. It's going great.

Gravedigger lifts up easily – brilliant, a sky wheelie!

But I'd flipped the front up too high. It wasn't going to land right...

Gravedigger was turning over and there was nothing I could do...

CRASH!

Emergency crews rushed to see if I was OK, but the seatbelts, helmet and roll cage had protected me completely. I was fine.

And elated too! I'd caused about £5,000 worth of damage, but that's nothing in the world of monster trucking. I'd done a sky wheelie, and even if I hadn't landed it quite right, I knew that I was a hero.

A monster hero!

11

SETH GETS

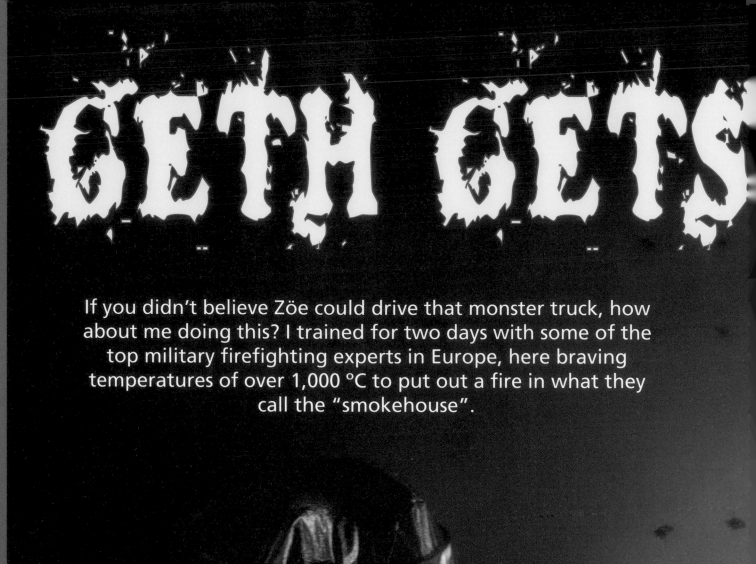

If you didn't believe Zöe could drive that monster truck, how about me doing this? I trained for two days with some of the top military firefighting experts in Europe, here braving temperatures of over 1,000 °C to put out a fire in what they call the "smokehouse".

FIRED UP!

It's actually far harder to see what
you're doing than this photo indicates. At
times, the smoke was so dense I could barely see my
hands. And the massive face mask meant I wasn't really
aware of anyone else in there with me. I felt very lonely,
and pretty scared.

When I first arrived, one of the key things I had to get right was my breathing equipment. The seal on my mask needed to be 100% perfect to stop me breathing in poisonous smoke, so it was only when I passed what's called a "fit test" that I could go any further.

Then I tried on my shiny silver heatproof suit – with our cameras recording every moment. If the fire trucks look a bit different from normal, that's because I was being trained by the US Air Force firefighting department based at RAF Mildenhall in Suffolk. Almost everyone I met was American!

My preparation included carrying heavy ladders, dragging fire hoses, and, here, cutting open a car to rescue people inside. I also had to get used to wearing my protective suit and safety equipment. Altogether, it weighed nearly 50kg – over half my bodyweight.

At least there was a bit of time to see the more glamorous side of the job. Who wouldn't want to ride in a fire truck like this?!

Pictures: Karen Abeyasekere

Finally, after two days, it was time for my biggest test – and it wasn't something to be taken lightly, as you can see from the size of the safety briefing.

The biggest fear for these guys is aircraft fires, so they've built one of the world's largest mock aircraft on which they can practise fighting fires. And now it was my turn....

With flames roaring high above me, I led my two firefighting buddies towards the mock aircraft. As we carried the huge fire hose, we sprayed water up, down and around the blaze. It was an exhausting few minutes, but eventually, the fire was over.

And so, sadly, was my training. I'd learnt a lot over the past couple of days, but most of all I had a new respect for the skills and bravery of firefighters everywhere.

ON A WING

Flying ace Zöe and flying ace Andy checking in for duty - sir!

Blue Peter presenters have always been famous for trying out mid-air stunts, and this was no exception! Zöe and I were each strapped to the outside of an airplane so we could perform a synchronised dance-like routine high in the sky – something that's called "wingwalking".

AND A PRAYER

WINGWALKING started in America in 1918, when lots of young flying aces returned from the First World War needing to earn money. They used their skills to wow audiences with incredible aerial stunts – including getting out of the cockpit and walking on the wings of their planes.

Nowadays, you aren't allowed to walk on the wings for safety reasons, so you're strapped in to a harness instead. But there's a special mechanism which still allows you to swivel around, and as I practised my moves on the ground, my adrenaline was definitely starting to pump!

We were about to perform our mid-air routine, climaxing in the legendary "mirror manoeuvre". This was an unbelievably difficult move involving touching hands while I was upside down. How would we fare? Turn the page to find out…

FACTBYTE

The first-ever wingwalker, Ormer Locklear, died in 1920 while filming an aerial stunt for a Hollywood movie.

Oh my goodness, it was a totally breath-taking experience. The power of the wind rushing against our faces and bodies was incredibly strong, and made it very hard to talk (something we always have to do for the Blue Peter cameras!).

I loved it – it felt like "surfing in the air".

Zöe just focused on being as graceful as possible!

As for our routine, it was going great! We performed almost all our moves at exactly the same time. But how about the show-stopper: the upside-down mirror manoeuvre…?

We did it! Well, almost. The air turbulence was so great that at the key moment it kept the planes apart. But our positioning was perfect, and we were ready to touch. Our instructors were in no doubt that, if the wind had been a bit lower, we would definitely have held hands. Overall, they were delighted with how we'd done – and so were we.

THE WHITE CLIFFS

No, those aren't computer graphics. These images from our opening titles really do feature our world-famous ship logo painted at the top of the equally-famous White Cliffs of Dover. This is the story of how we did it.

7am. I arrived at South Foreland Lighthouse at the top of the White Cliffs, overlooking the English Channel, not knowing what I was doing, or why.

Designer Nancy Jacks soon told me. My task was to paint the Blue Peter ship in a grassy field so it would be big enough to see from the air. But it wouldn't be normal sized, oh no. Instead it would be over 30 metres tall!

Fortunately, Nancy had already traced out the outline of the logo in the grass. But with just one roller, it was going to be a long task, and I had less than a day to do it.

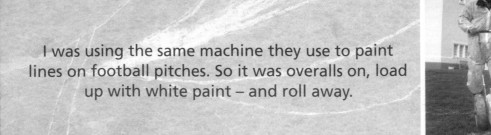

I was using the same machine they use to paint lines on football pitches. So it was overalls on, load up with white paint – and roll away.

`08:00`

`12:00`

`14:00`

I wasn't making a lot of progress. There was a lot of ground to cover and the machine wasn't easy to use. If Tony Hart, the artist who originally designed our logo, was watching, what would he make of it all?

Then Nancy had another surprise for me. The cliffs and the lighthouse belong to the National Trust, and schools are frequent visitors. She'd arranged for a group of children to turn up and give me a hand. Boy, was I relieved!

It was just in time. The filming helicopter was due to fly over mid-afternoon, and with minutes to go, we made it! Nancy and I took turns celebrating in the middle. We've been able to see our handiwork on TV at the start of Blue Peter almost ever since. It's just a pity the logo itself was painted in environmentally-friendly wash-off paint. Two weeks later, it was gone.

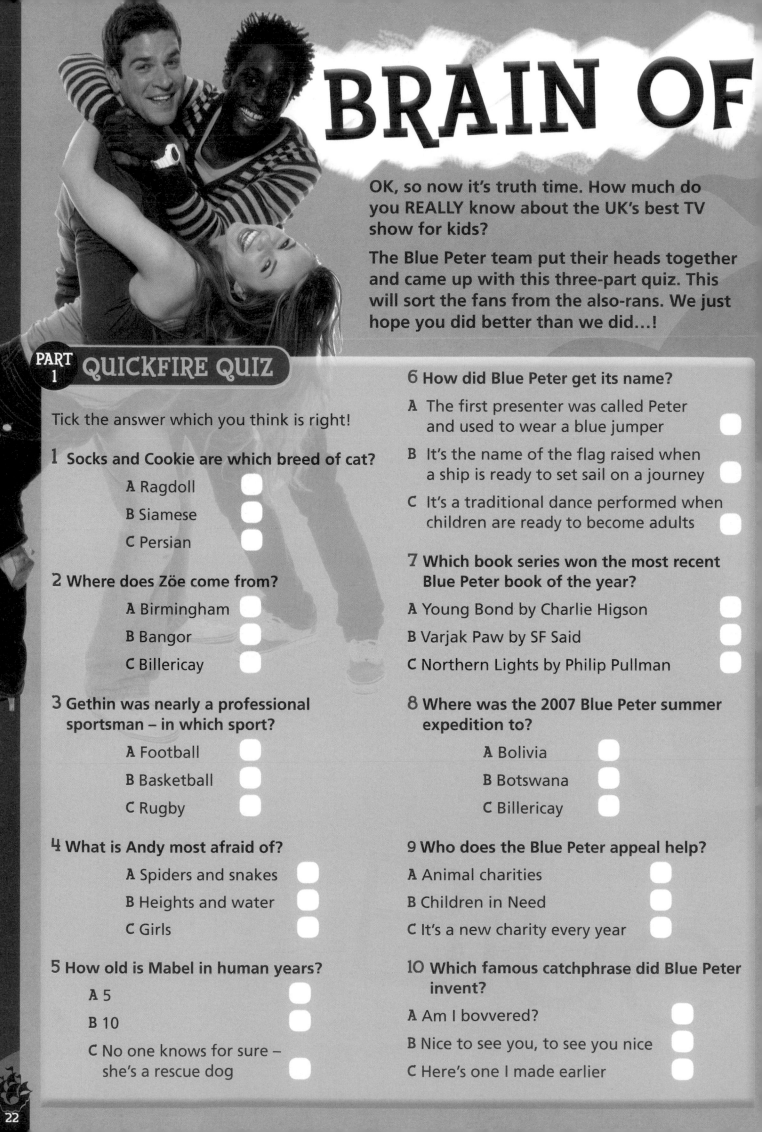

BRAIN OF

OK, so now it's truth time. How much do you REALLY know about the UK's best TV show for kids?

The Blue Peter team put their heads together and came up with this three-part quiz. This will sort the fans from the also-rans. We just hope you did better than we did…!

PART 1 QUICKFIRE QUIZ

Tick the answer which you think is right!

1 Socks and Cookie are which breed of cat?

A Ragdoll

B Siamese

C Persian

2 Where does Zöe come from?

A Birmingham

B Bangor

C Billericay

3 Gethin was nearly a professional sportsman – in which sport?

A Football

B Basketball

C Rugby

4 What is Andy most afraid of?

A Spiders and snakes

B Heights and water

C Girls

5 How old is Mabel in human years?

A 5

B 10

C No one knows for sure – she's a rescue dog

6 How did Blue Peter get its name?

A The first presenter was called Peter and used to wear a blue jumper

B It's the name of the flag raised when a ship is ready to set sail on a journey

C It's a traditional dance performed when children are ready to become adults

7 Which book series won the most recent Blue Peter book of the year?

A Young Bond by Charlie Higson

B Varjak Paw by SF Said

C Northern Lights by Philip Pullman

8 Where was the 2007 Blue Peter summer expedition to?

A Bolivia

B Botswana

C Billericay

9 Who does the Blue Peter appeal help?

A Animal charities

B Children in Need

C It's a new charity every year

10 Which famous catchphrase did Blue Peter invent?

A Am I bovvered?

B Nice to see you, to see you nice

C Here's one I made earlier

Blue Peter

PART 2 · SCRAMBLED HEADS

Who are these famous guests who've joined us on the show over the past year?

PART 3 · WEIRD WORLD

We've tried out all kinds of different challenges this year – some crazy, some just completely new to us. Can you fill in the missing letters to identify the activity?

C ☐ E ☐☐ ☐ EA ☐ ING

BEA ☐ BO ☐ ING

☐ E ☐ LY ☐ A ☐ CING

☐ NDER ☐ A ☐ ER C ☐ ☐ LING

P ☐ ☐ ZA SP ☐ ☐ ☐ ING

FAN RATING

Now add up your scores and write in your total here:

0-8: **Fairweather friend** You enjoy Blue Peter but have obviously missed out on loads of good stuff. You need to set your box to record the show automatically!

9-14: **Voracious viewer** Good work! You are rocking on in there with your Blue Peter fandom. Keep it up in 2009, and spread the word!

15-20: **Supporter supreme** Are you a mind-reader? What an incredible score – you are the greatest! We reckon you should come and join the team....!

Part 3: Cheerleading, Beatboxing, Belly dancing, Underwater cycling, Pizza spinning
Part 2: Richard Hammond, Same Difference (with their mum), Miss Piggy, Ade Adepitan, Geri Halliwell
Part 1: 1a, 2b, 3c, 4b, 5c, 6b, 7b, 8a, 9c, 10c (used by presenters when they jump a stage during a studio "make")
You get one point for each right answer.

NOW YOU SEE IT

If, like us, you ever need to keep something secret, this is exactly what you need! The sneaky spy book looks like a normal folder, but has a hidden second section to conceal notes and messages. We've also got a recipe for invisible ink. Now, what do we need to hide from Zöe...?!

MATERIALS:

For the spy book

4 rectangular pieces of card
(each 10.5cm by 15cm)
3 pieces of ribbon
(each 20cm long by 5cm wide)
Glue
Wrapping paper
Labels or stickers

For the invisible message

Bicarbonate of soda
(diluted in a little cold water)
Paintbrush
Ballpoint pen and paper
Red cabbage leaves
Hot water
Heat-proof jug or bowl

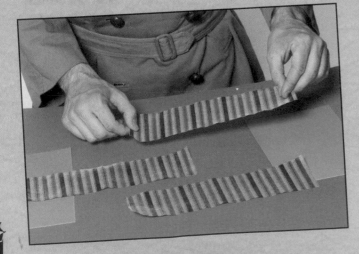

TO MAKE THE SPY BOOK
STAGE 1

Lay down two pieces of card side-by-side and place the three strips of ribbon between the cards as shown. If you make a larger spy book you will need wider ribbon to cover it top-to-bottom. Glue one end of one ribbon strip to the middle of one piece of card. Glue the other two strips of ribbon at the top and bottom of the second piece of card.

MAKE IT!

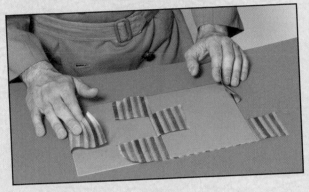

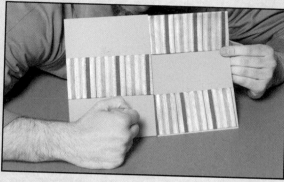

STAGE 2

Tuck the long ends of the ribbon strips under the opposite piece of card and glue the loose ends down.

STAGE 3

The ribbons will then be in neat strips on the other side of the card.

STAGE 4

Fold the cards in half with the neat side on the inside.

STAGE 5

Cover the other two pieces of card in wrapping paper and stick one on each side of the spy book to cover the outside.

STAGE 6

Decorate the outside with a label or stickers, making sure that you encourage people only to open the book one way.

To make an invisible message

STAGE 1

Put a few red cabbage leaves in a heat-proof jug or bowl and carefully pour on some very hot water. Put the cabbage leaves to one side while the water cools.

STAGE 2

While you are waiting, put a spoonful of bicarbonate of soda into a small bowl, add a little cold water and stir until the powder has dissolved. Using a paintbrush, write a secret message with the liquid on a piece of white paper.

STAGE 3

To disguise the secret message once it has dried, use a ballpoint pen to write a false message over the top.

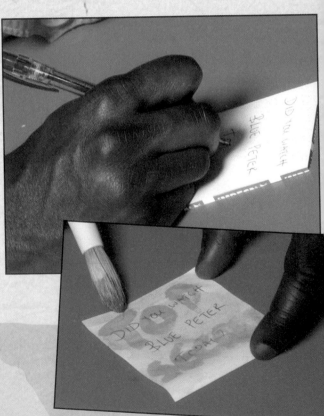

STAGE 4

When the red cabbage juice has cooled down, remove the leaves and paint some juice over the paper and the secret message will reveal itself! Be quick though – the message will disappear very quickly.

To hide your secret notes

STAGE 1

Open the spy book the wrong way round and place your message in the centre between the ribbons.

STAGE 2

Close the spy book and turn it over.

STAGE 3

Open the spy book normally, and the message will seem to have disappeared. In fact, it will be hiding under the centre ribbon on the other side.

TA-HA, FOOLED YOU!

27

STAT STACK

Born: Ibadan, Nigeria

Date of birth:
30 November 1983

Family:
Three brothers, one sister

Previous job:
Runner for CBBC

ALL ABOUT ANDY

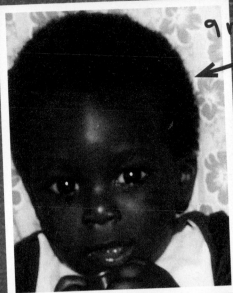

9 months old

MY EARLIEST MEMORY

Crying when my parents dropped me off at school for the first time. We had a nanny at home and I just wasn't used to so many people around. But almost immediately I made a couple of friends and it was OK.

Me with my brothers in Nigeria

WHAT I WAS LIKE AT SCHOOL

Quite cheeky! But my teachers liked me and I got away with a lot.
- Favourite subjects: English and PE.
- Worst subject: Woodwork – I was just bad at making things.

Me and my mum

Cooking!

MY MOST EMBARRASSING MOMENT

When I dressed up as a pantomime dame for Blue Peter. It was with Christopher Biggins, and it just wasn't me. I've never felt so stupid in all my life!

MY HOPES FOR THE NEXT YEAR

To keep travelling and meeting different people, and to go on some great adventures with Helen and Joel. I hope – and I'm sure – I'll have as good a friendship with them as I did with Gethin, Konnie and Zöe.

BOLIVIAN
road trip

BOLIVIA

This definitely isn't quite what it looks like – but then Bolivia isn't exactly what you might expect either. This South American country was the destination for our summer expedition, and what we did and saw was, well, extraordinary.

Possibly the most eye-opening sight was the Salar de Uyuni salt flat. At over 4,000 square miles, it's almost half the size of Wales. It's so flat and smooth that your eye can't really work out the perspective, so by combining objects that are near and far away, you can have all kinds of fun taking impossible-looking pictures. As we did!

FACTBYTE

At 3,640 metres, Bolivia's La Paz is the highest capital city in the world

The Salar de Uyuni was created when, thousands of years ago, an even bigger lake dried up, leaving a flat bottom made of salt. Altogether, there's at least 10 billion tons of the white stuff. Less than 25,000 tons is dug out each year, and after our measly go, make that about 25,000.1…

As you'd expect, the salt is sold for cooking. But that's not its only use. We also stayed at a salt hotel, where the building and furniture are almost totally made of blocks of salt. You even sleep on a bed made of salt!

And as if all that wasn't extraordinary enough, there was just time to sample a local tradition: a cleansing salt bath. Doesn't exactly seem like Zöe's cup of tea....

FACTBYTE

Spain ruled Bolivia for over 300 years

31

"Joy is pain, and pain is joy".

Never do I want to hear those words again! That was the slogan that Gethin and I were told over and over again when for two days we took on one of our most extreme football challenges ever.

The Tahuichi Way is a football academy with a difference. Each year, about 3,000 boys and 400 girls come to train here. The unusually tough regime is designed to improve football skills and stamina. But the academy also trains street children, and for some, it will help them leave behind their lives on the streets forever.

Geth and I started with exercises on an ordinary Bolivian football field – running, jumping, nothing you wouldn't expect. It was when we took to the massive sand dunes of Santa Cruz that things got tough.

If you've ever tried running through soft sand, you'll know it's not easy. But when it's in thick sand, uphill, and you're trying to kick a ball too - that's when it became something quite different; something quite epic. Geth and I went up and down, up and down. The longer it went on, the more exhausted I got.

Particularly when I hurt my calf. I didn't think I'd make it through the training.

But Geth and I worked together. Even when he finished one of the runs several minutes ahead of me, he was still there, cheering me on.

At the end of the two days, Gethin and I played a match against each other. I lost (just!), but it didn't matter. What the Tahuichi Way had taught me is that supporting each other is more important than victory itself. Oh, and **"joy is pain, and pain is joy"** ...

That wasn't all that we got up to in Bolivia. A lot of the country is covered in thick jungle, and we spent a night surviving on our own. Gethin rather proudly built us this shelter to sleep in – and somehow we coped!

As my guide showed me, you can eat some of the termites, even when they're still alive. They taste of mint!

This monkey took a shine to Zöe when she visited an animal sanctuary. Monkeys, chimps, bears and parrots can all be mistreated when they're kept as pets or as performing animals, so sanctuaries like this are life savers.

Bolivia is rather weirdly influenced by British traditions - particularly in the headgear department. Andy joined a carnival band, who all wore bearskins like the Queen's Foot Guards.

And, as Konnie found out, although llamas are farmed widely in Bolivia for their milk, meat and wool, they're also valued for their poo. When it's dried, it can be burnt as a fuel to cook food.

We loved Bolivia! It was beautiful, dramatic, and there were loads of things we'd never seen or done before. It was one of our most memorable expeditions ever. If you ever fancy being intrepid, we reckon it can't be beaten!

SPEED

How we went green for an eco marathon

Take one standard 24 volt electric wheelchair motor. Add two rechargeable batteries, a metal frame, a plywood cover, two Blue Peter presenters, and what have you got? A race-winning car? It may sound a bit unlikely, but ours was actually one of 25 electric racing cars which entered the first-ever Greenpower Corporate Challenge.

The four-hour race was all about encouraging schools to get involved in engineering by building eco-friendly cars, so we hooked up with a top team from West Somerset Community College. They did us proud! The car looked great, and when we met at Goodwood Motor Circuit on race-day, our hopes were high.

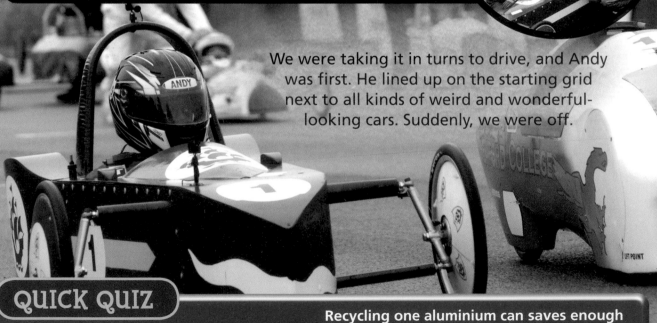

We were taking it in turns to drive, and Andy was first. He lined up on the starting grid next to all kinds of weird and wonderful-looking cars. Suddenly, we were off.

QUICK QUIZ

Which of these car features saves the most fuel when switched off?

⬜ In-car DVD ⬜ Air conditioning

The Tesla Roadster electric sports car can travel how long before being recharged?

⬜ 125 miles ⬜ 250 miles

Recycling one aluminium can saves enough energy to power a car radio for:

⬜ 3 minutes ⬜ 3 hours

Can electric cars be recharged in an ordinary plug point?

⬜ No ⬜ Yes

Answers: See the bottom of the next page.

DEMONS!

We started well, but then, on lap seven, disaster struck. An electrical connection came loose and Andy was forced to stop. He was furious! The car had to be towed back to the pits, and it took half an hour to fix the problem. We lost valuable time.

Fortunately speed-queen Zöe took to the wheel, and she happily started overtaking other cars. But the winner would be the car that covered the most miles in the time. Going too fast might mean we faded more quickly. It was all about tactics.

In the end, we had neither enough speed nor staying power. We finished 20th, having driven 80 miles in four hours. It was OK, but we knew that if we hadn't broken down, we might have got into the top ten.

Big congratulations to the winners, Seaford College, who drove their car, The Phoenix, an incredible 122 miles. With an average speed of just over 30 miles an hour, it's not exactly Formula One – but it goes to show that, when it comes to driving, batteries can sometimes be included.

Flower Power

I love giving my mum presents, but normally I'm really stuck for ideas, especially on Mother's Day. I've done the daffodils and I've done the chocolates, and, anyway, you know what mums always say: "Oh, I really love it when you make something for me!" So why not take them up on it? We've come up with something that's free, that's fun to do, and reuses what would probably normally be rubbish.

PS Yes that really is a photo of me with my mum when I was just a baby!

MATERIALS

To make the flowers
Coloured supermarket plastic bags
Green pipe cleaners or wire wrapped in green paper
Ball of modelling clay

To make the photo box
2 clear plastic CD cases
The holey middle section from another CD case
Sticky tape
Coloured or decorative tape
Piece of card
4 photographs

STAGE 1

Cut four rectangular pieces from plastic bags and lay them on top of each other. They need to be the same size, for example 10x15cm, in any colour combination you like.

STAGE 2

Start folding the sheets in a concertina fashion, making each fold about 1cm wide.

STAGE 3

Hold the folded strip together in the centre while you round off both ends using scissors.

STAGE 4

Wrap one end of the pipe cleaner or green-covered wire around the centre of the folded strip. This makes the stem.

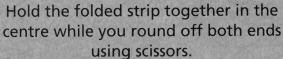

STAGE 5

Fan out the strip on both sides of the stem. Separate and spread out each individual sheet of plastic so that they fill out into a flower shape.

STAGE 6

Make more flowers of varying colours. Bunch three or four together and join them by winding one of the stems around the others. If you want a really big display, make four bunches.

To make the photo box

STAGE 1

Open the empty CD cases and stand them so that the four sides form a square. Tape them together at the sides using clear sticky tape.

STAGE 2

Cut a piece of card to fit into the base of the box and tape in place.

STAGE 3

Slot one photograph into each side of the cube, using the semi-circular tabs on two of the sides and the solid clip-in pieces on the other sides.

 STAGE 4

Take the extra holey section and tape one edge to one side of the top of the box. This acts as a lid so that you can change the photos.

STAGE 5

Stick coloured tape around all sides of the box to cover the clear sticky tape and make a sturdy box. Hey, there's that picture of me and my mum again!

STAGE 6

Lift the lid and push a bunch of flowers through each hole. Mould a lump of modelling clay around the stems to weight them inside the box. You could put an extra single flower through the centre hole to make it look really special. Give it to your mum and bask in the glory as she coos at your creation!

ALL ABOUT ZOË

I can't believe I'm leaving Blue Peter after nearly four years. It's almost impossible to choose my favourite moments, but here goes...

HIGHEST

My sky-diving jump for Sport Relief was definitely my highest moment, in more ways than one.

FIRST DAY

It's a tradition that Blue Peter presenters audition on a trampoline, and I was no exception.

TOUGH

I learnt how to waterski, but not any old waterskiing, oh no. This was barefoot waterskiing!

TOUGHEST

This was definitely the hardest thing I had to do - run the London Marathon, all 26 miles of it.

COLDEST

For some reason, the producers loved putting me in cold climes, here spending a night in an igloo I'd built myself.

ULTIMATE MOMENT

For the Shoebiz Appeal, I went to Malawi to spend a night with children living with the disease Aids. The heart-wrenching bravery of the children will stay with me forever.

I'm truly sad to be handing over to another lucky presenter, but happy they're going to see the world. And now, it's goodbye from me. The world is waiting

I'll see you out there!

If there's one thing that Konnie and I love, it's living a life of luxury. But this being Blue Peter, when we were sent to the Caribbean islands of the Bahamas, we knew we'd do far more than chill by the poolside....

BAHAMIAN BLISS

I was given the amazing opportunity to take part in the Junior Junkanoo – the biggest annual festival on the island for children. It's a feast of music, dance, rhythm and costumes, and the children at AF Adderley Junior High were keen to show me all the right moves.

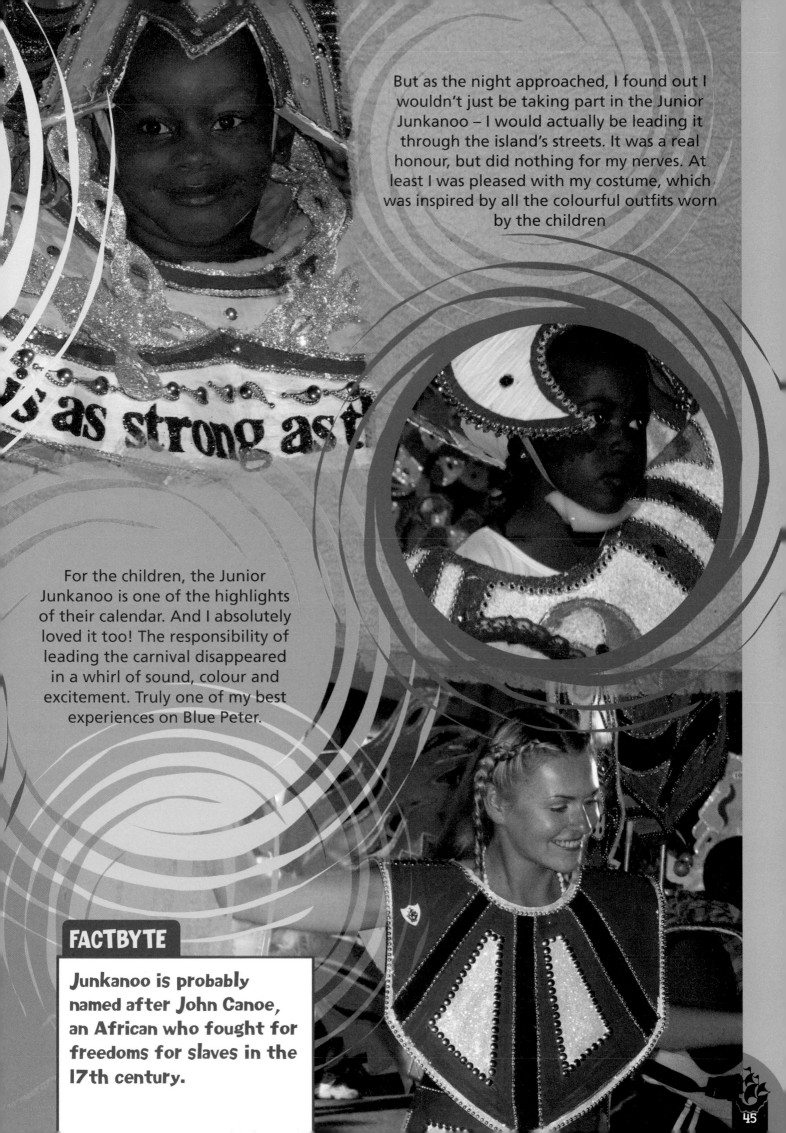

But as the night approached, I found out I wouldn't just be taking part in the Junior Junkanoo – I would actually be leading it through the island's streets. It was a real honour, but did nothing for my nerves. At least I was pleased with my costume, which was inspired by all the colourful outfits worn by the children

as strong as t

For the children, the Junior Junkanoo is one of the highlights of their calendar. And I absolutely loved it too! The responsibility of leading the carnival disappeared in a whirl of sound, colour and excitement. Truly one of my best experiences on Blue Peter.

FACTBYTE

Junkanoo is probably named after John Canoe, an African who fought for freedoms for slaves in the 17th century.

Konnie's trip involved something a whole lot scarier. Her challenge: to feed sharks by hand. Yes, you read that right – feed sharks, swimming in the open water, with bits of fleshy fish just centimetres away from her body.

As you can imagine, she had to do lots of training as soon as she arrived. She had to get comfortable with her special diving mask, and more importantly, to wearing a heavy chainmail suit. This would stop the shark's teeth getting through if they decided to sink them into her rather than into the fish.

Konnie did two test dives to get used to her heavy gear. And even though she was 15 metres underwater, with sharks swimming all around, she still managed to talk effortlessly into camera. What a pro!

Sharks have a bad press. They rarely attack humans, unless they are provoked. These sharks, Caribbean Reef Sharks, are some of the most gentle, and actually quite used to humans. One even bumped Konnie on the leg!

It was only on Konnie's third dive that she was finally allowed to put the raw fish on a feeding pole. It took a few minutes for her to pluck up the courage to hold it out far enough, but as soon as she did, the sharks started diving in to snatch the food away. She loved feeding these beautiful, fascinating creatures: an awe-inspiring way to end the trip.

FACTBYTE

Sharks attack fewer than 100 people a year.

The Highlands of Scotland was the unlikely location for one of my most space-age challenges ever: to launch Blue Peter's very own rocket.

Our hi-tech masterpiece was designed and created in specialist workshops in Cheshire. But launching rockets is a pretty dangerous business, so it had to be taken apart and reassembled hundreds of miles away, in the middle of a beautiful but deserted moorland.

I was working with Britain's top rocket builders – and if all went well, this would be the fourth-biggest rocket ever to be launched from Britain's soil.

Seeing our creation in position was a truly awe-inspiring sight. It was so tall, it was bigger than a house! And just before take-off, I got the chance to climb the launch tower to check all was OK. We were good to go!

3...

2...

1...

We have lift-off!

Our baby fired into the sky at several hundred miles an hour

What a triumph! It went exactly as planned.

For a rocket experiment really to succeed, it doesn't just need to take off; it needs to come down safely as well. And it did just that, using its onboard parachute, with only one fin smashed on landing.

STAT STACK

Rocket height: 7.4m

Altitude reached: 1km

Top speed: 300mph

Cost: £10,000

Fuel: Nitrous oxide and rubber

Blue Peter's very first rocket – ahhh, it makes me very proud!

GETH'S BEST BEACH BAG EVER!

MATERIALS

Lots of plastic milk bottles
(you can get 2 squares from
4 pint bottle)
Hole-punch
Coloured bag-ties, ribbon or st
Clear plastic tubing or ribbon
(for the handle)
Tape
(masking tape is good as it's ea
to remove)
Pencil and ruler

I'm a pretty outdoorsy type of guy, and I reckon this bag is perfect for the beach. Because it's made of panels tied together, the sand just drops through. And it's so light, you could pack it if you're flying abroad for some winter sun!

STAGE 1

Mark out the largest squares you can on the sides of the milk bottle and cut them out. The bigger the bag, the more squares you'll need.

STAGE 2

Make a pencil mark in each corner of each square – this helps stop you punching too close to the edge (which is easier than you might think!

STAGE 3

Punch the holes in the corners of the squares.

Lay the squares on a table with the sides just touching. Use pieces of masking tape to hold the squares in place, to help you with the next stage.

STAGE 4

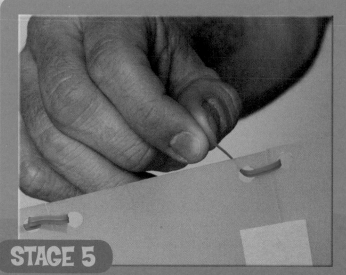

STAGE 5

Link the squares together by threading bag-ties through the holes, and press them neatly in place. For a different look, you could link the squares using short lengths of ribbon or string or even a paper clip.

STAGE 6

Remove the tape and make the other side of the bag. Now make a strip of plastic squares that's long enough to fit down one side, along the bottom, and up the other side.

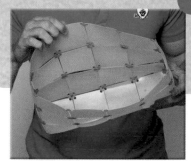

STAGE 7

Join the sides together using your strip of squares.

STAGE 8

Now decide what kind of handles you'd like. One solution I like is to thread coloured string through a length of clear plastic tubing.

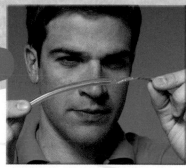

And finally, do as Spice Girl and children's author Geri Halliwell did when she helped me make this bag on the show, and just pop in your gear and off you go. She told me that she'd definitely be taking the bag out with her. I reckon that's a bit of a celebrity seal of approval!

STAGE 9

Then tie the ends of the string through the holes at the top of the bag. You can make the handles as long or as short as you'd like.

52

ALL ABOUT GETHIN

I've had such a brilliant time on Blue Peter, and there have been hundreds of highlights. It's been really hard to choose, but here are just a few.

FIRST DAY

It may have been raining in the Blue Peter garden, but I was the proudest man on earth!

HEROES

I trained with champion boxer Joe Calzaghe - one of many stars I've been lucky enough to meet.

ADVENTURE

I've travelled the world for Blue Peter, and in Japan I trained as a Samurai warrior.

HAVE A GO

Many of my top moments have been sporting challenges, including learning how to wrestle.

SHOWBIZ

I didn't realise I'd have to sing quite so often - here on our awesome Christmas special, Totally Blue Peter.

ULTIMATE MOMENT

This was without a doubt my toughest challenge: the Royal Marines Commando Yomp. The gruelling eight-hour marathon nearly broke me. At the end, I was in tears.

Thanks to everyone who's supported me over the past three years! I've really had a ball, and whatever I do and wherever I go, a part of Blue Peter will always be with me.

OUR MISSION: TO TAKE PART IN SPORT RELIEF 2008

OUR CHALLENGE: TO CLIMB THE TALLEST PEAKS IN EACH OF THE FOUR NATIONS OF THE UK

OUR DEADLINE: JUST TWO DAYS TO DO IT!

TREK TO THE TOP

DAY ONE: MORNING

Our trek started at 5am with what we thought would be the quickest mountain. But Slieve Donard took us three hours to climb – and that was just going up. This wasn't going to be as easy as we thought.

At least the views from the top were astonishing. Although she's from Northern Ireland, Zöe had never climbed the peak before, and she vowed to come back – with her mum and dad.

DAY ONE: AFTERNOON

We had beautiful weather for the climb up Snowdon, and Gethin very appropriately got to the summit first. Not just his home country, but his 30th birthday too! But once again, the climb down took ages, and we finished in the dark.

BEN NEVIS **1,344 metres**

SCOTLAND

NORTHERN
IRELAND

SCAFELL PIKE **978 metres**

SLIEVE DONARD
849 metres

SNOWDON **1,085 metres**

WALES

ENGLAND

DAY TWO: MORNING

Our legs and knees were starting to ache, and the rocky terrain of Scafell Pike didn't help. But we were determined to keep going – with Andy catching a few personal memories along the way.

DAY TWO: AFTERNOON

We'd climbed the first three peaks, but we were a couple of hours behind schedule, and it was touch-and-go whether we would have time to climb Ben Nevis. Then a sudden disaster put paid to all our plans.

The helicopter taking us to Scotland developed a technical fault and had to land miles away. The climb was off. As we watched the sun set, we knew we wouldn't make our goal.

DAY THREE: MORNING

But next morning, we were refreshed and ready to go. Encouraged by our team leader, Ben Major, we decided to take on Ben Nevis anyway. In the most exhilarating weather imaginable, "The Ben", as Scottish climbers call it, was something we didn't want to miss out on.

Ben Nevis is considerably higher than the other peaks we'd climbed, and in order to cope with the ice, we had to put on crampons: spiky boots that grip the surface.

With good equipment and a great team spirit, we eventually had the satisfaction of reaching the top – even if it was a day later than planned.

TREK TO THE TOP: How it was done

So how did we manage to climb all our peaks in, well, not two days, but a-little-over-two-and-a-half days?

The answer: sheer determination, and a little bit of help from some friends.

Here's what the TV cameras didn't show you – the three of us, getting up at 5am, definitely not looking our prettiest.

Each morning we had to pack our rucksacks with food, water and essentials…

…and until the sun rose, we used torches to show us the way.

We were very fortunate that the Royal Navy had a Merlin helicopter which flew us and the camera crew between the mountains – something which seems to have made Gethin very happy…!

Getting into and out of the jump suits may not have been the most elegant thing we've ever done, but once airborne, the view was definitely worth it.

And so was the chance to catch up on some
much-needed sleep!!

EXTREME RUGBY

The toughest game on earth just got tougher!

Hopefully you know by now that I love rugby, so when I heard about the most extreme rugby tournament on earth, I nagged and nagged the Blue Peter producers, until finally they agreed to let me take part.

The Artic Rugby tournament is held each year in Saariselkä in Finland, 100 miles north of the Arctic Circle. That means it's very cold, and very very snowy.

I joined a squad called the Warriors from the Finnish capital Helsinki. Six teams entered the two-day international tournament, playing seven-a-side rugby, instead of the normal 15 for rugby union. But most of the rest of the rules were the same.

The big difference was playing on snow – which made things ten times tougher. It was harder to run on than grass, physically more tiring, and it hurt when you fell (ahhhhh, poor me!).

The Warriors got off to a great start! We won our first game against English side Kingsclere 19-4, and then whopped Rovaniemi from Finland 44-0.

I was on storming form, kicking a load of points and even scoring a couple of tries (there's me in the orange jersey crossing the line, if you look hard enough!). I nearly turned professional when I was younger, and it was great to be playing full-on rugby again.

After five games, we were elated: we'd made it to the final. But then some bad news. We were facing the Gingermen from Ireland, the only team we'd lost to in the previous stages. We knew we had a fight on our hands.

But we played hard and ran out 24-12 winners. The lads on my team were all great, and it was a brilliant feeling to get my hands on the trophy, even if it was made of reindeer antlers. Oh well, I suppose at least it was appropriate...

World Tour

We've been right round the world this year to bring you the weirdest and most wonderful sights and experiences on the planet. Can you work out where the countries we've visited belong on the map?

**BOLIVIA NIGERIA CHINA PORTUGAL
FINLAND USA BAHAMAS EGYPT**

CELEB WORDSEARCH

Over the past year, loads of celebrities have appeared on Blue Peter, whether it's been to take part in our events, help our appeal or just hang out with us in the studio.

We've often given them Blue Peter challenges to take on. So why not take us up on this challenge too, and find their names – and ours too – in this fiendish wordsearch!

ANDY   **GETHIN**   **ZOE**   **DAVID TENNANT**

SCOTT MILLS   **LEE MEAD**   **DICK**   **DOM**

MCFLY   **MATT LUCAS**   **SUPER MARIO**   **SHAYNE WARD**

ALESHA DIXON   **ANTHONY HOROWITZ**

E	T	H	O	Z	O	Q	P	Y	D	D	V
A	N	B	M	A	T	T	L	U	C	A	S
S	D	I	A	N	Z	F	E	D	I	V	F
W	V	G	F	S	C	L	A	T	Z	I	Y
R	Z	L	E	M	G	E	N	H	X	D	C
S	B	H	B	T	M	C	T	Q	N	T	W
H	U	O	G	E	H	D	H	A	P	E	N
A	N	P	E	W	X	I	O	S	U	N	M
Y	K	L	E	D	I	X	N	C	J	N	T
N	S	S	E	R	B	V	Y	G	E	A	N
E	B	C	W	W	M	C	H	E	I	N	N
W	A	O	O	Z	S	A	O	D	P	T	O
A	R	X	F	T	U	Z	R	Z	I	K	H
R	J	Q	Y	X	T	I	O	I	D	C	W
D	V	G	N	C	F	M	W	W	O	O	K
A	L	E	S	H	A	D	I	X	O	N	M
T	E	T	H	D	K	T	T	L	E	L	J
C	I	Z	G	S	Z	N	Z	F	L	Y	O
K	N	N	H	O	R	L	E	X	E	S	Q

BEHIND THE SCENES

What really happens in the Blue Peter studio

The studio morning normally starts with make-up. Not just for the girls, though – the boys also have to have powder on their faces, otherwise the hot, bright studio lights would make them look shiny and sweaty. **NICE!**

Then it's on to the studio floor for rehearsals. There are hundreds of lights, most of them hanging from the studio ceiling. As well as making the set colourful, they also ensure we don't appear dark and shadowy.

There are normally four cameras in the Blue Peter studio, but because they move fast, it can seem like there are more.

One of the things that studio visitors love most is meeting the pets. They are very friendly and adore the attention! They're only brought on to set at the very last minute by their "pet handlers". Leonie, who's standing up here, has been looking after the dogs for longer than anyone can remember!

Just before we go live, our producer and his team discuss final changes to the script and running order. We rehearse each show for about three hours to make it as exciting, as clear and as entertaining as possible.

Filming in the garden is always very special – but it's no less complicated, with lights, camera tracks and cables everywhere. There are about 30 technical crew who are needed to make every edition of Blue Peter. Hopefully it looks easy and calm on screen, but behind the camera, it's normally anything but!

THE STORY OF BluePeter

So we've done it! It's incredible to think it, but this year, Blue Peter celebrated its fiftieth anniversary. We're officially the longest-running children's magazine show in the world, and here's our certificate from Guinness World Records to prove it.

It's all a very, very, veeeeeeerrrry long way from 16 October 1958, when Christopher Trace sat down in a suit and tie and said he would "show you what's new in the things which specially interest you younger viewers, boys and girls".

Blue Peter really became famous when the "dream team" of Peter Purves, Valerie Singleton and John Noakes got together in the mid-1960s. Along with the legendary pets, they drew in eight million viewers every edition – as much as the big soaps and talent shows do today.

They weren't the only household names: Biddy Baxter was editor for an amazing 22 years and helped create the formula that proved so popular.

Over the years, a magic mix came together which made up the Blue Peter that most people love and remember. It included:

The appeal, which gave children a chance to help other people around the world.

Makes and bakes, including these Christmas tree cards made by presenter Janet Ellis.

Competitions, with amazing prizes, and the chance to meet presenters like Sarah Greene, Peter Duncan and Simon Groom.

Badges, as pinned on by presenter Lesley Judd. Listening to children has always been crucial for Blue Peter.

Daredevil stunts, such as this record-breaking four-mile jump by Blue Peter's longest-serving presenter, John Noakes.

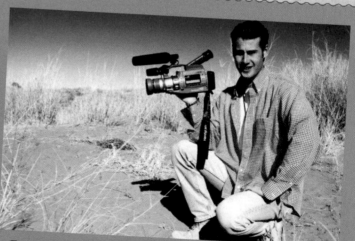

Foreign adventures, including the summer expedition, here with 1990s presenter Tim Vincent

Blue Peter has also helped create some of the most famous moments in TV history.

The Blue Peter garden, including the famous Italian sunken garden, hit the headlines when it was vandalised three times between 1978 and 1983.

The presenters have buried several time capsul over the years, and when we dug two of them in 2000, it seemed like the whole world wante to see what was inside. Sadly, only a few of th items survived intact.

This is perhaps the most famous moment of all. On 2 July 1968, Lulu the elephant caused mayhem in the studio. She pooed and weed all over the floor, and then, as her keeper tried to get her under control, she pulled him over. Chaotic moments like this might not be so unusual nowadays, but at the time it was a sensation.

Mark Curry, Caron Keating and Yvette Fielding, with Bonnie the dog. Sadly, Caron died of cancer in 2004.

So far, Blue Peter has had over 30 presenters and 20 pets. If you don't recognise some of them, your mum or dad might!

Diane-Louise Jordan (Blue Peter's first black presenter), John Leslie and Anthea Turner.

Stuart Miles, Katy Hill, Richard Bacon (who was sacked for taking drugs in 1998) and Romana D'Annunzio.

Matt Baker, Konnie Huq (Blue Peter's longest-serving female presenter, with over ten years on the show), Simon Thomas and Liz Barker.

To find out who the two new Blue Peter presenters are turn to page 104!

CHALLENGE TIME!

Over the past year, we've been set all kinds of challenges to take on during the show. Some of them we've practised beforehand, and some have been surprises – hence the blindfold. Here are a few of our favourites. And if you've got ideas for what challenges you'd like us to take on, why not let us know?

In April, to mark the Sikh New Year festival of Vaisakhi, we invited one of Britain's top bhangra dance troupes to put Geth through his paces. And his funky moves proved that he was more than just waltz and tango. Anyone for Strictly Come Bhangra?

This one was a surprise for Konnie, but the challenge was for Andy. He had to give her the ultra-fashionable beehive hairstyle – as seen on Marge Simpson, Amy Winehouse, and our very own Zöe Salmon. He was assisted by celebrity hairdresser Daniel Galvin Jnr (far left) and his chief stylist Brendan Fowles.

QUICK QUIZ

Vaisakhi is also a harvest festival

TRUE   FALSE

The beehive was invented in the 1950s

TRUE   FALSE

Answers: See the bottom of facing page

Sometimes we took our live challenges out of the studio. Andy and Gethin were blindfolded for two hours before pasting up a massive billboard advertising our on-air times. Nice picture, shame about how the words ended up...

We've always known how brave Zöe is, but even we were impressed when she walked on scorching hot coals in the Blue Peter garden. The reason it worked included walking so fast her feet didn't touch the coals long enough. But Zöe was trained and monitored by professionals, and this stunt can go wrong, so please don't try it at home!

Photos: Ed Jasion/BLAZE Firewalking

A-Z OF WEIRD

This was one of our most fun features from the whole year – so take a trip through our alphabetical zoo and find out all about the world's craziest critters. And why don't you choose your weirdest animal by giving each one a score out of ten?!

A is for Aye-Aye

Not only does its face look strange, it also has an unusually long middle finger which it uses to get grubs out of wood. From Madagascar (an island off Africa).

Score ☐

B is for Bearded Dragon

When threatened, this lizard creates a spiky black pouch under its chin which looks like a beard. From Australia.

Score ☐

C is for Chinese Crested Dog

Originally from Africa, these dogs got their name centuries ago when they were taken on ships to China to catch mice.

Score ☐

This was my weirdest animal, because it's not Chinese at all!

D is for Degu

This small rodent can lose part of its tail when escaping from enemies. From Chile.

This was my fave because I loved what it can do with its tail!

Score ☐

E is for East Indian Wandering Whistling Duck

Instead of quacking, this duck makes a call like a whistle. From Asia.

Score ☐

F is for Fly River Turtle

This underwater turtle has a nose that looks like a pig – though we're not entirely sure why! From Papua New Guinea.

Score ☐

ANIMALS

G is for Ghost Mantis

This extraordinary insect looks like a dead leaf, and grows to only about 5cm long. From Madagascar.

Score ☐

H is for Hog-Nosed Snake

Another one with a nose like a pig, but this time we know what it uses it for: it's a kind of shovel to help it dig in sand. From North America.

Score ☐

I is for Iguna

These large lizards can grow up to 2m long and are eaten in some countries – where they are called "chicken of the trees". From Central and South America.

Score ☐

J is for Jackass Penguin

It gets its name from its shrill mating call, which sounds a bit like a male donkey, a jackass.

From Africa.

Score ☐

I liked this the best because of the weird noise it makes!

K is for Kookaburra

This large kingfisher also makes a weird noise: its call sounds strangely like human laughter. And it steals meat from barbecues! From Australia

Score ☐

L is for Livingstone's Fruit Bat

Its thick reddish fur and dog-like muzzle mean it's sometimes called a "flying fox". From Africa.

Score ☐

M is for Meerkat

This small sociable animal is the first non-human mammal that's been seen actively teaching its young.
From Africa.

Score ☐

N is for Nephila Spider

This amazing spider spins webs that shine like gold in sunlight. The female is huge, about the size of a human hand, but the male can be up to 1,000 times smaller.
From Africa.

Score ☐

O is for Okapi

The zebra-like camouflage stripes on its rear legs help the young follow their mother through the rainforest.
From Africa.

Score ☐

P is for Potoroo

This marsupial is like a rabbit-sized kangaroo, and is now endangered because people used to eat them.
From Australia.

Score ☐

Q is for Quetzal

The favourite food of this brightly-coloured tropical bird is wild avocado, which it swallows whole, stone and all. From Central and South America.

Score ☐

R is for Red-Eyed Tree Frog

Its bright eyes are a defence mechanism: by opening them suddenly, it scares off predators.
From Central America.

Score ☐

S is for Scheltopusik

This lizard looks like a snake because it has no legs; but it's not a snake because it has ears and eyelids.
From Southern Europe.

Score ☐

T is for Two-Toed Sloth

This furry sloth spends most of its life hanging from trees, and when it has to move, it takes about three hours to travel a mile.
From South America.

Score ☐

U is for Upside-Down Jelly Fish

It has hundreds of tiny "mouths" with which to feed itself.
From the Caribbean.

Score ☐

V is for Victoria-Crowned Pigeon

Unusually for a bird, it produces milk to feed its young. From Indonesia.

Score ☐

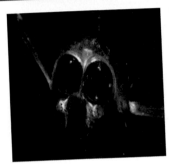

W is for Winteria

This bizarre deep-sea fish lives up to two kilometres underwater, and has enormous tubular eyes to help it see in the dark.
From the Pacific and Indian Oceans.

Score ☐

X is Xenopus Frog

This frog has a small flattened head – and because of the way it reacts to hormones, it's been be used to test if women are pregnant.

Score ☐

Y is for Yemen Chameleon

This large green chameleon changes colour depending on its mood, going a bright olive-red colour if scared. From the Middle East.

Score ☐

Z is for Zebra Shark

This shark only has zebra stripes when it's young; they turn into leopard-like spots as it gets older. From the Pacific and Indian Oceans.

Score ☐

My weirdest animal is:

Because:

HALF A MILLION DISCS!

The story of the Disc Drive appeal

Sarann and Danny were the faces of our latest appeal – but the Disc Drive was about far more than them.

Sarann is 9 and loves music and dancing. But her mum can't see well. Sarann spends several hours every day looking after her and helping round the house.

There are nearly 200,000 young carers in the UK. Young carers are children who look after someone they're close to (often a mum, dad, brother or sister) who is ill, disabled or has problems with drugs or alcohol.

Those children often miss out on their childhood, on the fun things that most children take for granted. They may also need extra support to do well at school.

Danny is also 9. He's already saved his mum's life over 100 times! His mum has a severe form of diabetes, and he gives her the treatment she needs, sometimes in an emergency.

BluePeter

DISC DRIVE

Helping Young Carers in the UK · **Barnardo's**

We asked you to help by collecting as many discs – CDs, DVDs, computer games – as you could, which Barnardo's sold in their shops to raise money. And to launch the appeal in style, we got in Shayne Ward and Matt Di Angelo to help us break a world record.

We decided to topple as many discs as we could. We flew in the world domino-toppling experts from the Netherlands, and there were two days of careful, painstaking preparation.

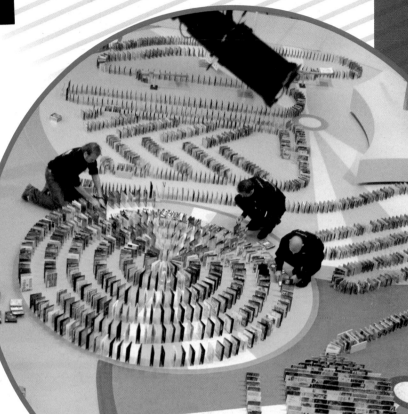

There were even CDs going up the stairs to our treehouse!

But it all went brilliantly, and we broke the record – over 2,000 discs toppled in all.

A great start!

But what really mattered was what happened next. And you didn't let us down! Within just a few weeks, tens of thousands of discs were pouring in. Already, we were providing young carers with afterschool clubs, days out, advice sessions and support groups. You were doing us proud.

For Sarann, things were about to get a lot more exciting. Andy had already spent a day at her home to give her a break from the daily routine. Now he wanted to surprise her with something even more special – a trip to Egypt, her dream destination.

As she looked at the pyramids and rode a camel for the first time in her life, she knew this was a once-in-a-lifetime opportunity.

Sadly, most young carers won't get breaks as dramatic as Sarann's.

But her journey was a symbol of the difference that the Disc Drive can make for children across the UK.

We cared so much about the Disc Drive that we took every opportunity to promote it: radio, TV, newspapers, even the shops. Shortly before Christmas, we were invited to design a window display for a big department store using – yes, you guessed it – discs.

We were delighted with the result. The big, bold, modern design seemed to fit well with the shiny silver of the discs. The Disc Drive was really picking up speed!

But our hard work was nothing compared to what you'd been doing. Within three months, we were able to announce that you'd helped us break our target of 250,000 discs. In fact, we sailed past – by the summer you had collected more than half a million. It's a brilliant result and one that will change the lives of tens of thousands of children.

THANK YOU!

ME AND MY COSTUME DRAMA

Zöe's two-minute movie

One of the highlights of the year is definitely our Me and My Movie competition. It's a brilliant chance for CBBC viewers to make and upload short films – with one person winning a very special Bafta award.

So I decided to make my very own costume drama. Here's what I found out along the way…

STAGE ONE – PREPARE

1 WRITE A SCRIPT

Discuss it with a friend, who'll soon tell you if you're not making sense! And draw a storyboard to show which shots you need.

2 SORT OUT YOUR PROPS

Frilly dresses may not be your thing (!), but hunt through charity shops or your mum's wardrobe to get the look you want.

3 GET THE TECHNICAL SIDE RIGHT

OK, so I had a few pros on standby, but the more people who help out, the better – particularly if they're experts!

1 GET ON LOCATION EARLY

One of the biggest problems is over-running, so turn up early, with all your gear sorted out too.

2 BRIEF YOUR ACTORS

Make sure everyone's clear what you want – and don't be afraid to tell it like it is!

3 LIGHTS, CAMERA, ACTION!

Start filming. And, yes, I know I've got a massive crew, but, hey, I'm like a big Hollywood star (or something)…

4 SHOP FOR SNACKS!

If you're like me, you'll want to keep on going, but not everyone will feel the same. Have some supplies handy.

5 HANG OUT WITH SOME CELEBS.

Definitely, definitely rope in some star names. I got soapstars Matt Di Angelo and Gerard McCarthy. I'm sure you can top that…!

For more information about Me and My Movie, go to bbc.co.uk/cbbc. This year's competition closes on 6 October 2008.

INJURY

How Andy got a sca

Normally, we put a lot of time and effort into making sure we don't come to any harm on our dangerous escapades. But for one day only, we turned the tables, and Gethin gave Andy the most horrific injury you could imagine. Fortunately, it was only special effects – courtesy of the experts at Holby City.

Vicky Voller is the prosthetics make-up designer for Holby City. She creates all the show's artificial wounds and organs – including fake hearts and false arms. Vicky makes most of them using silicone, a soft rubbery substance, and the first thing she had to do was get the right colours to match Andy's skin. He had one of the darkest pieces in the box!

We knew that Vicky would be bringing in a selection of her award-winning work for us to look at. What we weren't expecting was to see a severed head sitting in a suitcase at the side of the studio. It was all a lot spookier than we had anticipated!

TIME
to shout about!

To demonstrate how lifelike the injuries can be, the show opened with blood apparently spurting out of Zöe's arm.

Gethin started making Andy's injury by painting the silicone mixture on to Andy's skin.

But Holby's Nurse Maria – played by actress Phoebe Thomas – soon revealed that it was all a trick. The wraparound arm pulled off, and we showed the fake blood being pumped from behind the scenes.

He created the gash by pulling the silicone apart with a lollipop stick, and poured in fake blood to complete the look. Does anyone else think Gethin is enjoying this just a bit too much?!

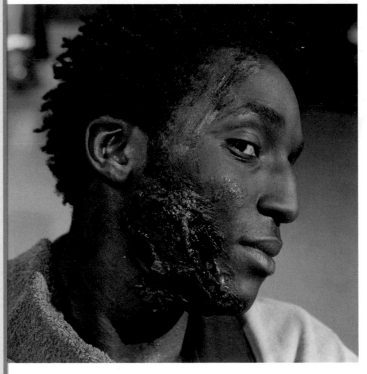

The final effect was pretty dramatic. Vicky pronounced herself to be very happy with Gethin's effort – even if we thought it looked a bit more like Andy had just had an accident with a burger and tomato ketchup bottle!

PUMPKIN RACING

Think you know about pumpkins? Think again! We hooked up with Britain's most successful giant pumpkin growers to try out one of Britain's newest, and barmiest, sports: pumpkin racing.

So how do you get pumpkins quite so massive? Every grower has their own secrets, but the key is to use a seed from one of last year's giant pumpkins. The very best can cost up to £100.

And then water it – a lot. Sometimes 100 litres a day. In its peak growing season, a giant pumpkin can grow 25kg a day.

By the time Konnie and I met the "Extreme Pumpkin Growers", their pumpkins weighed over 500kg and needed five of us to move them. And then it was down to business, turning them into, well, boats.

Once we'd cut the top off, I got busy scooping out the flesh inside my pumpkin to give me a nice comfortable place to sit.

Konnie, on the other hand, got out the power tools, getting everything ready to fix on the outboard motors which would drive the pumpkins through the water.

At last, the day of the big race. I had worried whether the pumpkins would float and stay upright, but once we put them in the water all seemed well, so with the help of my pumpkin grower Ian, I clambered aboard.

Konnie had sheer determination on her face. It being Halloween, mine was called "Trick" and Konnie's "Treat". But which would win? And would the pumpkins stay afloat. We were about to find out…

We were off! A huge crowd had turned out at Lymington, on the south coast of England, and they all wanted to see who would win this epic event!

But almost immediately disaster struck. We stayed afloat; but we couldn't control the circular pumpkin boats. They just kept turning round, and the more we powered them, the faster they spun. It all ended in chaos. Neither of us won the race – but at least we'd had fun finding out more about these amazing giant fruit.

Going Home

Andy travels back to Nigeria

You might know me as Andy Akinwolere, but that's not my full name. I was christened Odunayo, a name which comes from Nigeria, the African country where I was born. I moved to the UK when I was eight, and I've not been back to Nigeria since. So when Blue Peter suggested I visit my home country again, I leapt at the chance.

This is me with my Uncle Gbenga, both of us wearing traditional Nigerian outfits.

I was so excited about visiting my grandma, who I hadn't seen for 17 years. What I didn't expect was that she would lay on a colourful, noisy welcoming party, complete with local dance band!

We soon caught up about everything that had been happening in our lives. Like all grandmas, she thought I'd grown up into a fine young man – but, also like most grandmas, she told me off for my hairstyle, which she thought was too long!

Perhaps the most moving part of my visit was when I went to see where my grandad used to sleep and work. He was one of the leaders of the Methodist church in Nigeria, but he had died since I left the country. Looking at all his books, which were exactly as I remember them, I was overcome with emotion.

My family roped me in to getting ready for a celebration meal. I had to go to the busy market to buy some of the food we'd need. I picked up a yam, a fleshy vegetable that's grown all over Nigeria. I bartered with the stallholders to get the best deal, though I still think think I paid more than the locals!

FACTBYTE

Nigeria produces over 26m tonnes of yams a year - nearly two-thirds of the world's total.

My 12-year-old cousin showed me how to pound the yam – something that has to be done for several minutes. Some yams can make you ill if they're not prepared or cooked properly. She made it look so easy, but I struggled to do it right! We got there in the end, though, and cooked, it tasted delicious. We had a brilliant meal.

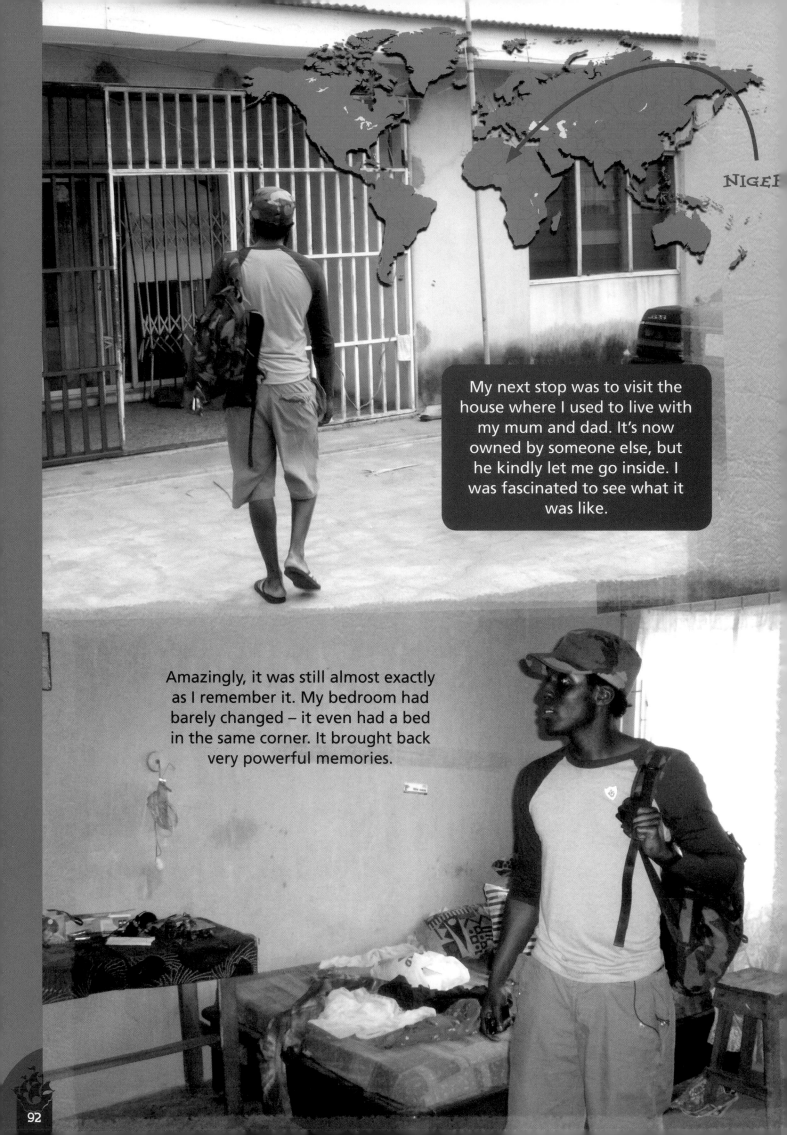

NIGE

My next stop was to visit the house where I used to live with my mum and dad. It's now owned by someone else, but he kindly let me go inside. I was fascinated to see what it was like.

Amazingly, it was still almost exactly as I remember it. My bedroom had barely changed – it even had a bed in the same corner. It brought back very powerful memories.

Everywhere I went, people seemed delighted to see me. I revisited my old church and my old school, and the children put on a real welcome. I explained that I now presented one of the most famous children's programmes in the UK, and they all cheered!

And check out these hairstyles!

Most Nigerian boys tend to have their hair short (not my palm tree style for them), but the girls have their hair plaited in an incredible number of ways. I loved spending time with them all.

QUICK QUIZ

Nigeria is bigger than Britain

☐ True ☐ False

The Nigerian flag is made of green and white stripes

☐ True ☐ False

Nollywood, the Nigerian film industry, is the third biggest in the world

☐ True ☐ False

Nigeria used to be controlled by the UK

☐ True ☐ False

Answers: See the bottom of the page.

Quick quiz answers: They're all true! Nigeria's population is about 140 million people, compared to 60 million in the UK, and it's nearly four times the size. It got its independence from the UK in 1960.

93

Before I left Nigeria, there was one final thing I wanted to do - and talk about saving the best till last!

The Argungu fishing festival is one of the largest in the world, with 20,000 people plunging into the Matan Fada river, to see who can catch the biggest fish.

It's a truly incredible sight, and the fish are pretty impressive too. They can weigh up to 75kg – as big as a grown man. Competition is fierce: the top prize is worth over **£17,000**, and includes a new car.

Unfortunately, it wasn't going to be me driving home! Even though I'd practised with traditional fishing nets, I didn't catch a single thing. But I didn't mind: I still had the memories of one of my most colourful and emotional journeys ever.

I got lessons from actor Barnaby Edwards (below), who's been working inside these mutants since Season One

GETH•IN WILL EX•TER•MIN•ATE!

We've got a great friendship with the guys at Doctor Who, but even I couldn't believe my luck when they asked me to... play a DALEK!

Each Dalek weighs about 20 stone, and although it's got supermarket trolley-style wheels, it's incredibly heavy to move. You sit inside on a wooden seat and kind of shuffle along, trying to steer it as smoothly as possible. You've also got to operate its head, ray gun and manipulator arm. It's nowhere as easy as it looks.

Before I started filming, I got some tips from the genius behind Doctor Who, scriptwriter Russell T Davies. He told me the key to operating Daleks was to remember that they're "mean, nasty and vile". He said I should act well "or I'll sack you".

No pressure then!

I chatted to Russell in the Monster Room where they keep the props – and before going onto set, I had a nose around. It was awesome seeing some of the scariest costumes in the galaxy just waiting around for their next appearance.

Be afraid, be very afraid of the **Pig Slaves** from Season Three's 1930s Dalek episodes.

Part man, part fish, Season Four's **Hath** are colonists from the planet Messaline.

The **Hoix** from Season Two • unusually seen with its mouth shut!

My starring role came during the second episode of the two-part season closer, Journey's End. I was one of two Daleks rounding up a group of human captives on board their mothership, Crucible. I had to move at exactly the right time, but I found it pretty difficult seeing out of the Dalek head, and set off too early.

Oh no – the whole crew had to redo the scene because of me. What would Russell say?! Fortunately, second time round I got it just right. Barnaby was delighted.

My short sequence still took two hours to film! It was fascinating seeing the care and effort that went in to everything. The set was made of wooden panels, but shining lights from outside created a convincingly eerie effect.

Clever TV tricks were used everywhere. These Dalek guards look pretty scary…

… but they're nothing more than pieces of plywood lit from behind.

My visit brought back happy memories of my previous visit to the set, when I was a Cyberman alongside the Doctor himself, David Tennant. So before saying farewell again, there was just time to catch up with a couple more of my Doctor Who friends.

John Barrowman, who plays Captain Jack.

Elisabeth Sladen, who plays Sarah Jane.

STAR-SPANGLED CHRISTMAS TREE

I love Christmas! I love the traditions, but I also like how it can be funky too – like this very modern tree. You can customise it how you want, and you could even make a bigger one to sit on the floor of your bedroom.

MATERIALS

Paper to make your pattern

Cereal boxes or sheet of card

Cardboard tube

Sticky-backed plastic or wrapping paper

Glitter, stickers or pom-poms

STAGE 1

Start by making a template for your tree. Draw a large triangle on paper and draw on stars as shown – including some overlapping the edge. The star patterns on this page may help. Cut out the template.

STAGE 2

Cover one side of a cereal packet with sticky-backed plastic or wrapping paper. Turn it over and place your template on the plain side. Draw round the template and cut out your tree.

STAGE 3

Cover the plain side of the card with more sticky-backed plastic or wrapping paper, and cut off the excess. Make a second tree in the same way.

STAGE 4

You now need to slot your two trees together to make your 3D tree stand up. To do this, make two slits in the trees – one cut from the top to the middle and the other cut from the bottom to the middle. Slot the trees together.

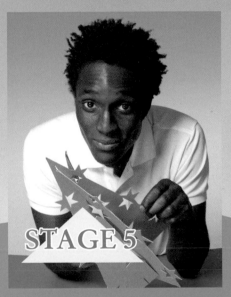

Make a Christmas tree tube using a 2cm ring cut from a cardboard tube. Cover it to match the tree and cut slits so the base slots into the tree.

STAGE 5

STAGE 6

To keep the tips of the tree together, use the largest star shape as a template and cut it out in card before covering it. Cut a cross slit in the centre of the star and push the tree through the slits.

Finally, personalise your tree even further with stickers, glitter or pom-poms. You can make it glitzy, shiny or just classily simple – it's all up to you!

101

COULD IT BE YOU?

Try our top presenter quiz!

With Geth and Zöe leaving, we were in the difficult – but exciting – position of finding two new people to take on "the best job in the world". Could YOU do it? Take our test to find out!

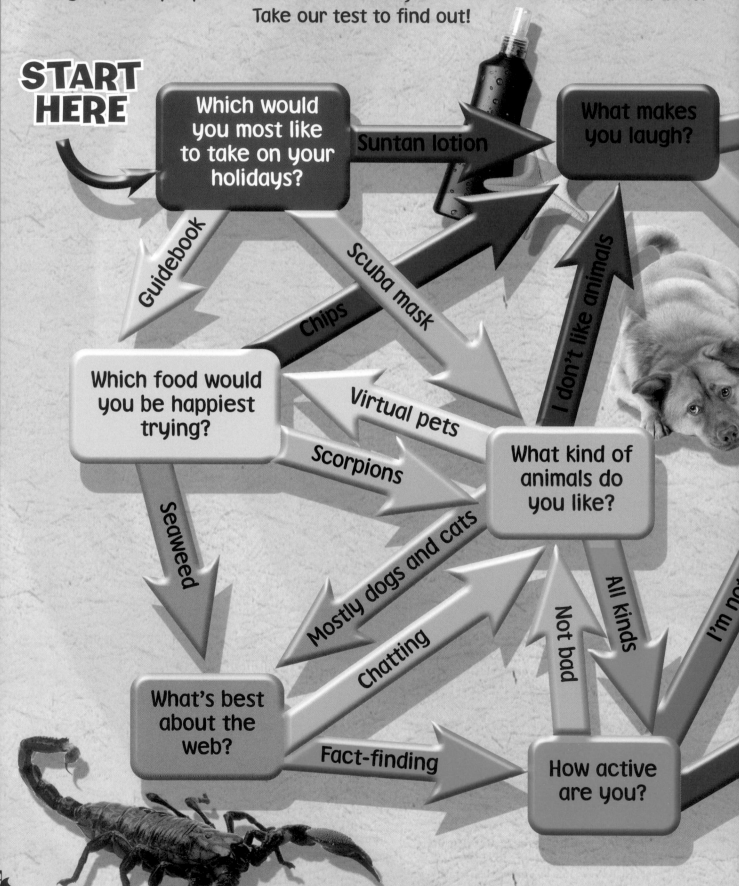

START HERE

Which would you most like to take on your holidays?

Suntan lotion

What makes you laugh?

Guidebook

Scuba mask

Chips

Which food would you be happiest trying?

I don't like animals

Virtual pets

Scorpions

What kind of animals do you like?

Seaweed

Mostly dogs and cats

Chatting

Not bad

All kinds

I'm not

What's best about the web?

Fact-finding

How active are you?

What do you like about Blue Peter?

I don't like it →

Nothing →

Everything! ↓

SORRY!
You haven't really got what it takes. And if you got here by answering just three questions, why are you even reading this?!

My friends →

Who would you most like to travel with?

Just me →

Best mate →

HMMMM – MAYBE...
You might be good, but you need to get a bit more excited about life. Have you thought about daytime TV?

What would most excite you about celebrities?

Reading about them →

Meeting them →

Pretty good →

YES – YOU'RE THE RIGHT STUFF!
If you got here by answering just four questions, even better. Keep going, and in a few years' time, it could be you…!

So who did end up replacing Geth and Zöe? Turn the page to find out…

Helen

STAT STACK

Born: Carlisle, England

Date of birth: 19 July 1983

Family: One older brother

Previous job:
Newsround reporter

ALL ABOUT HELEN

Almost one!

MY EARLIEST MEMORY

Going to watch my brother being a mascot at Carlisle United on a freezing cold day. I was about three or four and sat with my gran - and fell asleep!

I loved growing up on a farm (yes, those were my glasses!)

I also loved dancing

WHAT I WAS LIKE AT SCHOOL

I was so busy! I did a different activity every day, from netball and swimming to dancing.
- Favourite subjects: PE and French
- Worst subjects: Maths - my maths teacher used to let me make masks instead

Out of my teens - and those glasses

MY MOST EMBARRASSING MOMENT

Once I arranged to interview a top Government politician - but I waited at the wrong place. One hour later I realised my mistake and felt incredibly foolish!

MY HOPES FOR THE NEXT YEAR

That people will enjoy Blue Peter, and realise it's got a real value too. I want to see some incredible things - but I also want to get involved and help people.

Joel

STAT STACK

Born: London, England

Date of birth: 14 March 1985

Family: One older sister

Previous job: Music TV presenter in New Zealand

ALL ABOUT JOEL

Nearly two

MY EARLIEST MEMORY
Breaking a part on my parents' car, and hiding it and pretending to help look for it. I got away with it too...

Me aged ten, with a friend

WHAT I WAS LIKE AT SCHOOL

A bit cheeky, but enthusiastic too. And tiny! But suddenly I grew when I was 19, and now I'm about 5'11".
Favourite subjects: English and history
Worst subject: Science - I seemed to lack any ability to digest it, but now I want to learn!

Nearly four - and already being silly!

17, and feeling very grown-up

MY MOST EMBARRASSING MOMENT

I've had so many! On my music show in New Zealand, I once told a caller she'd done really well, and the caller said, "Um, I'm a guy". I had to joke about how his voice hadn't broken yet - but I'm still not sure if that was the case!

MY HOPES FOR THE NEXT YEAR

That I'll go on intrepid journeys around the world with Helen and Andy and see amazing things you wouldn't even imagine. I also want to learn more about myself: will I ever get so broken down that I'll cry on camera?

PET SUPERSTARS

One thing's always for certain with Blue Peter, our pets will always be the stars of the show!

Lucy and Mabel showed they still know where it's at when they modelled the latest fashion sunglasses for dogs. Stylish and safe: now there's something we should all be aiming for!

One of the most exciting moments of the year was when our latest kitten, Cookie, arrived. He joined us aged just 13 weeks, when he was still soooooooooo unbearably cute. He's definitely grown up a bit since then!

QUICK QUIZ
How many cats has Blue Peter had, including Cookie?
A 9   B 7   c 5
Ragdolls are particularly:
A Happy being indoors
B Active
Lucy is a pedigree:
A Golden Retriever
B Labrador
Answers at the bottom of the page

Like Socks, Cookie is a Ragdoll, and they live together too, so they get on famously. Which is pretty appropriate, seeing as they're probably among the two most famous cats in the UK.

We shouldn't forget Shelley, our tortoise. Shelley doesn't appear loads on TV, not least because she's in hibernation for a lot of the time we're on air. But we love her to bits, and whenever she's in the studio, it really feels like the Blue Peter family is complete.

CREDITS AND ANSWERS

Written by Tim Levell

Main photography by Chris Capstick

Makes by Gillian Shearing

Other photography Karen Abeyasekere, Andy Akinwolere, Mary Albion, Mike Cole, Sid Cole, Beckie Cooper, Tim Fransham, Damian Hall, Rob Howarth, Konnie Huq, Ed Jasion, Sarah Jeavons, Huw John, Gethin Jones, Oli Jones, Debbie Martin, John McIntyre, Jamie McLeish, Kara Miller, Gary Parsons, Mark Reynaud, Nikki Ryan, Kieron Schiff, Alex Sykes, Richard Turley, Nick Welch, Gerard Williams and Jamie Wilson.

Thanks to Kate Finburg, Jack Lundie, Audrey Neil, Melissa Hardinge, Sid Cole, Cath Gildea, Vanessa Clark, Ailsa Christie and the whole Blue Peter team for all their help and ideas.

The author has attempted to trace all copyright holders, but if an omission has been made, please contact us.

CELEB WORDSEARCH (p. 63) - Solution

E	T	H	O	Z	O	Q	P	Y	D	D	V
A	N	B	M	A	T	T	L	U	C	A	S
S	D	I	A	N	Z	F	E	D	I	V	F
W	V	G	F	S	C	L	A	T	Z	I	Y
R	Z	L	E	M	G	E	N	H	X	D	C
S	B	H	B	T	M	C	T	Q	N	T	W
H	U	O	G	E	H	D	H	A	P	E	N
A	N	P	E	W	X	I	O	S	U	N	M
Y	K	L	E	D	I	X	N	C	J	N	T
N	S	S	E	R	B	V	Y	G	E	A	N
E	B	C	W	W	M	C	H	E	I	N	N
W	A	O	O	Z	S	A	O	D	P	T	O
A	R	X	F	T	U	Z	R	Z	I	K	H
R	J	Q	Y	X	T	I	O	I	D	C	W
D	V	G	N	C	F	M	W	W	O	O	K
A	L	E	S	H	A	D	I	X	O	N	M
T	E	T	H	D	K	T	T	L	E	L	J
C	I	Z	G	S	Z	N	Z	F	L	Y	O
K	N	N	H	O	R	L	E	X	E	S	Q

HELLO! PICTURE QUIZ (p. 6) - solution

1 Konnie and Andy went along to wish Gethin well for his first show in Strictly Come Dancing – and they must have done something special, because he almost made it to the final. He finished third, after Alesha Dixon and Matt Di Angelo.

2 Zöe was challenged to create a modern painting that was good enough to hang in one of Britain's top art galleries, London's Royal Academy. This was her masterpiece, "Happiness".

3 Andy wasn't going to let Gethin beat him to the dancing crown: he tried out a new French craze, which involves dancing in the moving shovel of a digger.

4 For our look at Christmas traditions, Gethin spent a day at Santa School, where he learnt everything you need to be a stand-in Father Christmas. All together now: Dasher, Dancer, Prancer, Vixen...

5 Zöe braved what's called the "Wall of Death", in which motorcyclists ride their bikes horizontally around sheer vertical walls (relying on the twin forces of friction and centrifugal force to stop them falling down). Fortunately, she only had to ride on the handlebars!

6 Jake, our competition-winning cook, met almost every celebrity chef worth their salt during the year. Here, he cooked with Marco Pierre White, on board a new family cruise ship.

7 More food, and this time leading British film actor James McAvoy joined Andy in the studio for a bit of pancake tossing. We cooked weird pancakes from around the world, including seaweed and cabbage pancakes from Japan and shrimp pancakes from Nigeria.

8 This, believe it or not, is Zöe. To investigate the rise in obesity, a prosthetic make-up artist turned Zöe into a 32-stone woman for a day. Not many things make Zöe cry, but this did.

9 Sometimes it's so useful having double-height studio doors! An Iron Man came to visit us just before running the London Marathon in his nine-foot outfit. Lloyd Scott dresses up in crazy costumes to raise money for charity, and it took him five days to complete the 26-mile course.

10 These are the final 18 finalists in our Postcard to Beijing competition. Thousands of you entered our massive competition to find the young stars of the Olympic and Paralympic handover ceremonies in Beijing this summer. The two overall winners were Tayyiba and Gareth.